SPAIN
the land

Noa Lior and Tara Steele

A Bobbie Kalman Book

The Lands, Peoples, and Cultures Series

Crabtree Publishing Company

www.crabtreebooks.com

The Lands, Peoples, and Cultures Series

Created by Bobbie Kalman

Coordinating editor
Ellen Rodger

Production coordinator
Rosie Gowsell

Project development, photo research, and design
First Folio Resource Group, Inc.
    Erinn Banting
    Tom Dart
    Söğüt Y. Güleç
    Claire Milne
    Debbie Smith

Editing
Carolyn Black

Separations and film
Embassy Graphics

Printer
Worzalla Publishing Company

Consultants
Bredan Ara; Mike Ara; José Félix Barrio, Adviser, Ministry of Education, Culture and Sport of Spain; Isaac Hernández

Photographs
Esbin Anders/The Image Works: p. 5 (top); Roberto Arakaki/International Stock: p. 4; Xavier Catalan/Life File: p. 17; Corbis/Magma Photo News Inc./Tom Bean: p. 30 (left); Corbis/Magma Photo News Inc./Edifice: p. 3; Corbis/Magma Photo News Inc./Ric Ergenbright: p. 7; Corbis/Magma Photo News Inc./Robert Estall: p. 11 (top); Corbis/Magma Photo News Inc./Owen Franken: p. 6; Corbis/Magma Photo News Inc./Patrick Ward: p. 9 (bottom); Corbis/Magma Photo News Inc./Nik Wheeler: p. 11 (bottom); Sue Davies/Life File: p. 28 (right); Chad Ehlers/International Stock: p. 15 (bottom), p. 20 (left); Esbin-Anderson/The Image Works: p. 16 (top); M. Everton/The Image Works: p. 8 (top), p. 29 (top); Beryl Goldberg: p. 29 (bottom); Jose L. Grande/Photo Researchers: p. 31 (top); Blaine Harrington III: p. 14 (bottom); Isaac Hernández/Mercury Press International: p. 12 (top), p. 14 (top); Ronny Jaques/International Stock: p. 21 (bottom); Emma Lee/Life File: p. 5 (bottom), p. 8 (bottom), p. 9 (top), p. 13 (bottom), p. 19 (top), p. 20 (right), p. 21 (top), p. 23 (bottom), p. 26 (bottom); José Maza/MercuryPress.com: p. 12 (bottom); MercuryPress.com: p. 24 (both), p. 25 (both), p. 27; Allan A. Philiba: p. 10 (both), p. 15 (top), p. 19 (bottom), p. 28 (left); Mark D. Phillips/Photo Researchers: p. 26 (top); Loek Polders/International Stock: p. 22; Raga/Explorer/Photo Researchers: title page; Hans Reinhard/OKAPIA/Photo Researchers: p. 30 (right); Chuck Szymanski/International Stock: p. 16 (bottom); Paul Thompson/International Stock: p. 18 (left); Ulrike Welsch: cover, p. 13 (top), p. 23 (top); Terry Whittaker/Photo Researchers: p. 31 (bottom); Wysocki/Explorer/Photo Researchers: p. 18 (right)

Map
Jim Chernishenko

Illustrations
Dianne Eastman: icon
David Wysotski, Allure Illustrations: back cover

Cover: The entire city of Granada, in southern Spain, can be seen from a window in the Alhambra. The Alhambra is made up of the Casa Real, or royal palace; Generalife, the palace gardens; and the Alcazaba, a fortress.

Title page: Windmills and the ruins of an ancient castle line a ridge near Consuegra, a town in central Spain. The castle was built during the 1100s, and was once home to a group of Roman Catholic monks, or holy men. The windmills, which were once used to generate electricity, have been restored and are now shops and workshops for local artists.

Icon: Oranges, which are grown in many regions of Spain, such as Valencia, appear at the head of each section.

Back cover: The Hierro giant lizard lives in nature reserves such as the Coto Doñana.

Published by
Crabtree Publishing Company

PMB 16A,
350 Fifth Avenue
Suite 3308
New York
N.Y. 10118

612 Welland Avenue
St. Catharines
Ontario, Canada
L2M 5V6

73 Lime Walk
Headington
Oxford OX3 7AD
United Kingdom

Cataloging in Publication Data
Lior, Noa.
    Spain. The land / Noa Lior and Tara Steele.
    p. cm. -- (The lands, peoples, and cultures series)
    Includes index.
    Summary: Explores Spain's varied geography from the Cantabrian Mountains in the north to the southern Sierras and the vast rivers and coastal regions of the Atlantic and Mediterranean.
    ISBN 0-7787-9364-8 (RLB) -- ISBN 0-7787-9732-5 (pbk.)
    1. Spain--Description and travel--Juvenile literature. [1. Spain.] I. Title: Land. II. Steele, Tara. III. Title. IV. Series.
    DP43.2 .L56 2002
    946--dc21   2001047696
                                                           LC

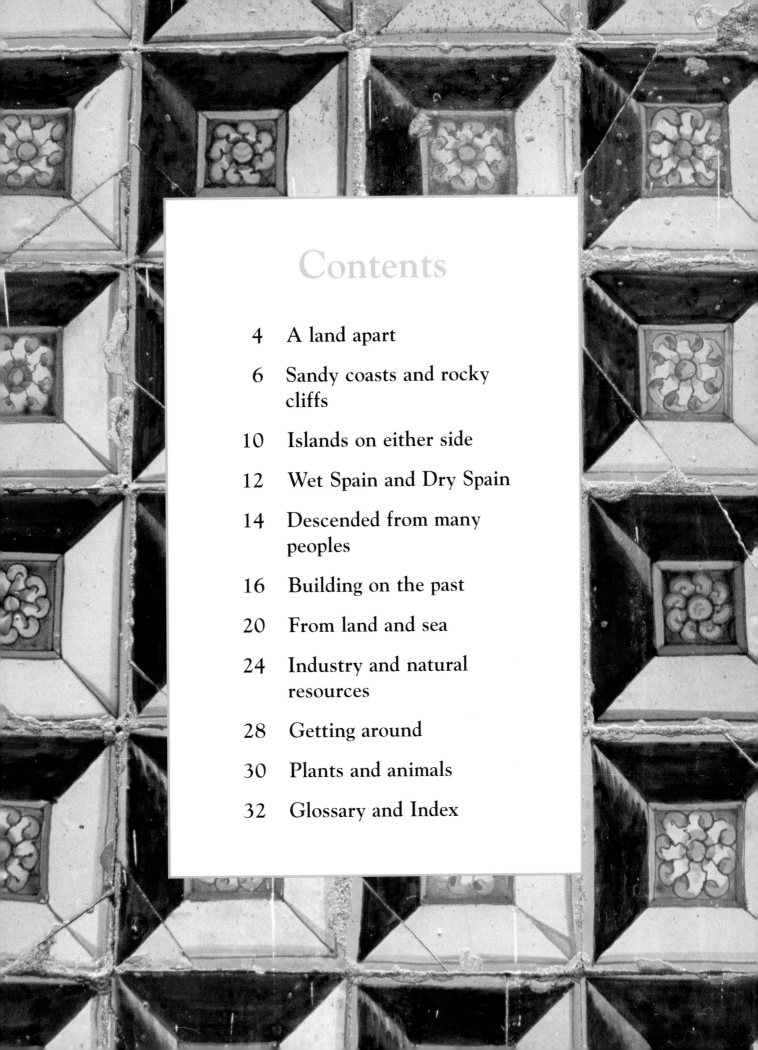

Contents

A land apart

Spain fills most of the Iberian Peninsula, a large chunk of land that forms the westernmost edge of Europe. The **peninsula** is almost completely surrounded by water. To the north, a chain of high and rugged mountains called the Pyrenees divides Spain from France. In the past, these mountains made contact between Spain and the rest of Europe difficult.

Spain is the third-largest country in Europe. It has **fertile** river valleys, sunny beaches, and hot, desertlike regions. Its varied climate and landscape mean that Spain has more types of plants than any other European country. While farming is still important to the country's economy, major industries such as car manufacturing and tourism now add to Spain's wealth.

Facts at a glance
Official name: España
Area: 194,884 square miles
   (504,750 square kilometers)
Population: 40 million
Capital: Madrid
Official language: Castilian
Main religion: Roman Catholicism
Currency: euro (as of January 1, 2002)
National holiday: National Day
   (October 12)

(top) The fertile farmland in Rioja, a region in northern Spain, is used to grow artichokes, beans, peppers, and grapes, from which the region's famous wine is made.

The Cibeles Fountain stands in front of the main post office in Madrid, the capital of Spain. During the civil war, which took place in the 1930s, the fountain was buried under sandbags to keep it from being destroyed.

The Guadalquivir River, or "Great River," flows through the city of Córdoba, in southern Spain.

Sandy coasts and rocky cliffs

Spain is a land of many regions, each with unique geographic features. **Plateaus**, beaches, mountains, and river valleys make it a richly textured land.

The central Meseta

The Meseta is a high plateau in the center of Spain that fills nearly half the country. Most of the red and yellow soil on the Meseta is dry and rocky, so only crops that do not require **irrigation**, such as wheat, are grown there. People on the Meseta also raise goats, pigs, and sheep. Few people live in the northern part of the plateau, but Madrid, in the south, is the most populated city in the country.

The Meseta takes its name from the Spanish word for table, *mesa*. Like a table, it is mostly flat. In a few places, though, rocky **outcrops**, low hills, and cliffs rise from the landscape. East of Madrid is the old town of Cuenca, which sits high on a steep cliff between two valleys. *Casas colgadas*, or hanging houses built from stone, perch on the edge of the cliff. Their wooden balconies look as if they are suspended in air. Hidden in the rough mountains near Cuenca lies the "Enchanted City," a group of rocks that the wind has carved into unusual shapes. Some rocks balance on narrow stems and look like mushrooms. One even looks like an elephant.

Many mountains

The Meseta is divided by a mountain range called the Central Sierras, and has mountains on almost all sides. To the north and northwest are the Cantabrian and Galician Mountains, with their peaks of pure **limestone**. The Iberian Cordillera, another chain of mountains, runs along the northeast and east, while the Betic Cordillera, the Sierra Morena, and the Sierra Nevada ranges are in the south. The snowy Pyrenees rise along the border between Spain and France.

*This **casa colgada**, which was built during the 1300s, towers above a rocky cliff in Cuenca, in central Spain.*

Andorra

Nestled in the Pyrenees is a country called Andorra. This country, with a population of only about 63,000 people, belongs to neither Spain nor France. Instead, it has two co-princes: the president of France and the bishop of Seu d'Urgell, which is the closest Spanish village to Andorra. An agreement made centuries ago dictates that in odd-numbered years Andorra sends the French co-prince a payment of money. In even-numbered years, Andorra sends the Spanish co-prince a payment of money, twelve chickens, six hams, and twelve cheeses! Today, the two co-princes have very little power. An elected parliament, led by a president, runs the country.

A small church stands near the village of La Vella, in Andorra.

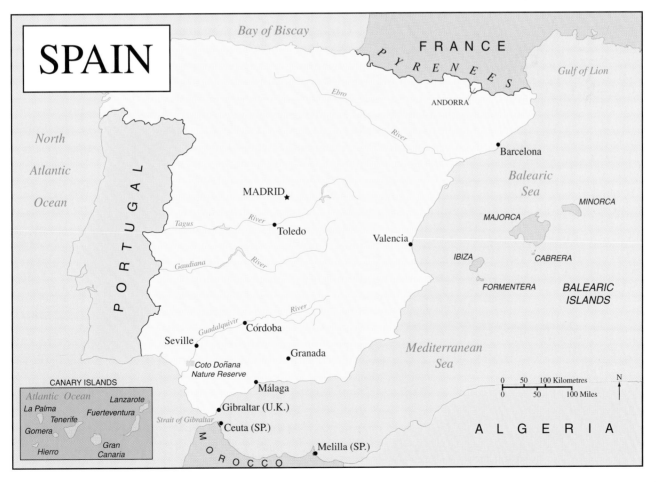

The coasts

The Atlantic and Mediterranean coasts of Spain are very different from one another. Huge waves batter the Atlantic coast, which has rocky cliffs and many *rias*, or inlets. By contrast, the Mediterranean coast is relatively calm, with long beaches of golden sand. The southern part of the Mediterranean coast is known as the Costa del Sol, or "Coast of the Sun." This area claims to have the greatest number of sunny days in Europe each year. Both Spaniards and tourists love the beaches of the Costa del Sol, which get very crowded in the summer.

Few rivers

Only a few major rivers flow through Spain: the Ebro, the Tagus, the Duero, the Guadiana, and the Guadalquivir. Some of the smaller rivers nearly dry up in the heat of Spain's long summer. Farmers use water from the bigger rivers, such as the Ebro and Guadalquivir, to irrigate the land, so they can grow fruit and vegetables.

This section of the sandy Costa del Sol will become crowded later in the day.

Houses dot the rolling pastures on the outskirts of Santillana, a small town in northern Spain. Santillana is in a region of Spain nicknamed "Green Spain." Rain and a mild climate help make this area perfect for farming.

The small village of Benimantel sits among the mountains of the Iberian Cordillera, in eastern Spain.

Gibraltar, Ceuta, and Melilla

Some land in Spain is not owned by the country, while some land in North Africa is owned by Spain. Gibraltar is a tiny peninsula near the southern tip of Spain. It has an area of just 2.3 square miles (6 square kilometers). Most of Gibraltar is made up of a huge limestone and **shale** ridge, called the "Rock." The eastern part of the Rock is very steep, while the western part slopes more gently. Gibraltar has not belonged to Spain since Great Britain took possession of it in 1704. Spain, however, still claims ownership of Gibraltar, and began negotiations with Britain in 1980 over the **sovereignty** of the small parcel of land.

The Rock of Gibraltar towers high above the Mediterranean Sea.

Spain holds five **territories** in northern Africa, including three small island groups and the coastal cities of Melilla and Ceuta in the country of Morocco. The Spanish conquered Melilla in 1497, and Ceuta became a Spanish territory in 1580. During this time, Spain also conquered many other lands, including Mexico, Peru, Portugal, and Cuba. After a while, these and other wars of conquest became long and costly, so Spain's power and influence on these countries declined. In the 1800s and 1900s, Spain lost most of its overseas territories, but continued to hold on to Ceuta and Melilla. Today, people in both these cities speak Spanish and Arabic, the language spoken by people who live in Morocco.

Spain owns two large groups of islands. The Balearic Islands are 120 miles (190 kilometers) off the east coast of mainland Spain, in the Mediterranean Sea. The Canary Islands are 620 miles (1,000 kilometers) south of Spain, 70 miles (115 kilometers) from the African coast.

The Balearic Islands

There are five main Balearic Islands, as well as many smaller ones. The five major islands, from largest to smallest, are Majorca, Minorca, Ibiza, Formentera, and Cabrera. They are a part of the Sierra Nevada mountain range that runs through southeast Spain. This mountain range begins on mainland Spain and continues into the ocean, where most of it lies underneath the water. The mountaintops that reach above the water form the Balearic Islands.

The islands have spectacular cliffs, sandy beaches, gently rolling hills, and fertile lowlands. The lowlands are perfect for growing citrus fruit, grapes, and olives. The mild Mediterranean climate and beautiful beaches have made these islands a popular tourist spot for hikers, cyclists, and swimmers.

The town of Ibiza towers above the city's main port, which is crowded with yachts and local fishing boats.

The Canary Islands

Millions of years ago, the eruptions of underwater volcanoes created the Canary Islands. When these volcanoes erupted, they spewed hot lava into the ocean, where it cooled and hardened. The lava slowly built up and created underwater mountains. Eventually, these mountains became tall enough to reach the surface of the water, forming the islands.

Naming the islands

The Canary Islands were not named after the small yellow birds that live there. Their name comes from the Roman word for dog, which is *canis*. Roman explorers called the islands *Canaria* because of the many large wild dogs they found there. The birds were then named after the islands, where they were first discovered.

Cape Formentor, a long strip of land on the northern coast of Majorca, reaches into the Mediterranean Sea. At the tip of the cape is a steep cliff that drops 650 feet (200 meters) into the sea.

The major islands

The seven major Canary Islands are Gran Canaria, Fuerteventura, Lanzarote, Tenerife, Gomera, La Palma, and Hierro. Each island has its own special features. Gran Canaria is marked by ravines, or deep valleys created by running water. Lanzarote is famous for its fields of hardened lava, which look like the surface of the moon. Tenerife is home to Spain's highest mountain, Pico de Teide, which is 12,198 feet (3,718 meters) high. La Palma is lush and green, while Fuerteventura is dry and desertlike. Hierro has mineral springs, while Gomera's freshwater springs irrigate the land where date palms grow.

Plants unlike anywhere else

The Canary Islands had no settlers before the 1400s, so their plant life was untouched for centuries. Over 2,000 different plants grow on these islands, and over 600 of them grow nowhere else in the world. Evergreen laurel forests that disappeared from the rest of the planet thousands of years ago can still be found on the Canary Islands.

*Tall stone sculptures called menhirs and cone-shaped structures called **talayots** stand throughout the countryside in Minorca, one of the Balearic Islands. Some of these monuments are more than 2,000 years old.*

Lanzarote's once fertile valleys were covered by lava during a series of volcanic eruptions. The first series of eruptions took place between 1730 and 1736. The last major eruption took place in 1824.

Wet Spain and Dry Spain

In January, Spaniards can swim in the ocean around the Canary Islands, off the southern tip of Spain, while their friends ski on one of the country's snowy mountains. The weather is dramatically different from region to region because of the varied landscape. Rain pours steadily on the northwestern coast, hot winds blow over the Meseta, and snow falls in many of the mountains.

In some parts of southern Spain, droughts are so severe that people are forced to abandon their farms and homes.

Wet Spain

Winds blowing over the Atlantic Ocean bring a lot of rain to Spain's northwest coast. This area is sometimes called "Wet Spain." Summers in Wet Spain are warm, **humid**, and rainy. Winters are cool and rainy.

Dry Spain

The central and southern parts of Spain are known as "Dry Spain." The central Meseta receives most of its rain in April. As the people who live there say, *"En abril, aguas mil"* or "In April, water by the thousands." After April, little rain falls. Summer is blistering hot, with dry winds that drift north from the Sahara Desert, in North Africa. These winds get trapped on the plateau by the surrounding mountains. The winter is bitterly cold, with below-freezing temperatures and sharp winds.

(top) In the northwestern region of Galicia, stone granaries called **horreos** *sit on stone stilts high above the ground, so dampness will not spoil the grain that is stored inside.*

Southern Spain

"The rain in Spain falls mainly on the plain" is a line from the musical *My Fair Lady*. It does not, however, describe the plains of southern Spain! Scorching winds from the Sahara blow over this area. As well, a wind called the *solano* brings broiling weather in the summer to the plains of Andalusia, in the south. This region is the hottest in all of Spain, with desertlike areas such as Almería, on the southern coast.

The Canary Islands

The Canary Islands are close to the Sahara Desert. Like the Sahara, they have hot and dry weather all year round, but pleasant breezes from the **Gulf Stream** cool off the islands in the evenings. The temperature changes very little from season to season, which makes the Canary Islands a popular spot for tourists.

Snowy mountains

Even in a warm climate like Spain's, some mountains are high enough to have snow on their peaks all year. Pico de Teide, on Tenerife, is permanently capped with snow. In the Pyrenees, the snow can be so heavy during the winter months that roads are sometimes blocked.

People from all over the world ski down the slopes of the Pyrenees.

In the south, snow covers the Sierra Nevada mountains for most of the year. These mountains are home to the southernmost ski resort in all of Europe. Skiers enjoy sliding down the slopes of the Sierra Nevada because of the warm and pleasant weather that awaits them at the bottom. World championship ski races take place on the highest mountain in this range, called Mulhacén.

Colorful umbrellas shield sunbathers on the crowded Levante Beach, on the southeastern coast of Spain.

Descended from many peoples

Over 100,000 years ago, people living in Spain decorated cave walls and ceilings with paintings that are still visible today. Over the centuries, these early people were joined by people from many parts of Europe and North Africa. Each group settled in a different area and developed its own **customs**. Mountain ranges and long distances made contact between these groups difficult. Today, there is more communication between people in different parts of the country. Most people speak Spain's official language, Castilian, and share many religious and cultural traditions. At the same time, they remain loyal to their distinctive, regional ways of life.

The central Castilians

For hundreds of years, the largest cultural group in Spain has been the Castilian people. Castilians live in the central provinces of Castilla-Léon and Castilla-La Mancha. A few still live in small farming villages, but the majority live in large cities with modern factories. One of the most famous legends told in Spain describes the battles of a noble Castilian, a soldier named El Cid.

Catalans

Catalonia, in northeastern Spain, is home to the Catalan people. Their language, also called Catalan, is similar to Spanish and French. It developed long ago from Latin, the language of the Romans. Since the 1600s, Catalans have fought for, won, and lost **autonomy**. In 1980, for the first time in years, they elected their own government.

A large family poses for a photo at a get together in Madrid. Mothers, fathers, children, aunts, uncles, cousins, and grandparents often live close to one another and spend a lot of time together.

Basques

The Basque people live in a region they named Euskadi, in the north of Spain and south of France. **Historians** believe that the Basques have inhabited their remote valleys since the **Stone Age**. They continue to preserve their ancient culture to this day. They speak a language called Euskera, which is unlike any other language in Europe. They also perform unique dances, songs, and sports. In the past, the Basques fought for, and partly won, the right to some autonomy. Today, some Basques continue to struggle for their own country.

Two boys, wearing traditional red hats and scarves, participate in a Basque festival in Pamplona, in northern Spain.

Galicians

Galicians live in northwest Spain, in the region of Galicia. They are descended from the Celts, an ancient people who came to Spain almost 3,000 years ago. Even after Romans conquered Spain in 200 B.C. and ruled for the following 600 years, Galicians held on to their traditions. They still play music on a Celtic instrument called a *gaita*, which looks like a bagpipe, and speak a language called Gallego.

People of Andalusia

When **Muslim** Arabs from northwest Africa, known as Moors, invaded Spain in 711 A.D., they came to Andalusia first. When they left Spain in the 1400s, they left Andalusia last. Many of the people who live in Andalusia today are **descendants** of the Moors. Andalusians developed bullfighting and created **flamenco** guitar music and dancing, which are famous throughout Spain and the rest of the world.

*(above) A man plays a **gaita** at a Celtic celebration in Mondoñedo, a town in northwestern Spain.*

(below) Friends gather in the Plaza de Santa Cruz, in the southern city of Seville.

❧ Building on the past ❧

Cars and people crowd the Gran Via, Madrid's main shopping street. The Gran Via runs through the center of Madrid, separating the old city in the south from the newer parts of the city in the north.

At the center of many Spanish cities are the remains of ancient towns, which were built by Romans, Moors, or early Spaniards long ago. Typically, a city's "old quarter" has narrow cobbled streets and small buildings that crowd together. Newer areas with wider paved roads, modern apartment buildings, and factories surround the old quarter. Madrid and Barcelona are Spain's two largest cities, home to about one-quarter of Spain's population.

Madrid, the capital

Madrid is the **capital** of Spain. In 1561, the Spanish king Philip II chose Madrid as the capital because it sat in the very center of the country. In fact, all distances on the nation's highways are measured from a marker, known as *"Kilómetro Cero,"* or "Kilometer Zero," at Puerta del Sol, an intersection in the center of Madrid where eight major streets meet.

*(top) On Sundays, many families go to the Retiro, in Madrid, to relax, enjoy a picnic, go for a **paseo**, or stroll, or row a boat in the lake near the monument to King Alfonso XII, who ruled Spain from 1874 to 1885.*

Culture in Madrid

Madrid has a vibrant culture. The people of Madrid, who are called Madrileños, enjoy going out to see films, plays, and concerts. When they want to see great artwork, they visit world-class museums, such as the Prado. The Prado houses important works of art that Spanish kings and queens collected over the centuries. Madrileños spend a lot of time outdoors in the summer. They eat in the city's cafés, relax on terraces, meet in beautiful public squares, or stroll by the lake and fountains in a very large park called the Retiro. *Retiro* means "retreat." The park, which covers more than 350 acres (142 hectares) in the middle of the city, was once a royal garden.

In many parts of Barcelona, modern buildings are sandwiched between offices, shops, and apartment buildings that were built hundreds of years ago.

Beautiful Barcelona

Barcelona is in northeast Spain, on the Mediterranean coast. It sits on a plain, with tall mountains on one side and the sea on the other. For over 2,000 years, Barcelona has been a major **port**. It is also the world's largest publishing center for books in Spanish, and the site of many conferences, exhibitions, and fairs every year. It hosted the Summer Olympic Games in 1992.

A famous **promenade** called Las Ramblas runs from the center of the city to the waterfront. *Rambla* means torrent, or swiftly flowing stream, in Arabic. Long ago, Las Ramblas was the sandy bottom of a stream outside the walls of the old city. In the dry season, when there was no water in the stream, Las Ramblas became Barcelona's main road. Butchers set up stalls there, and people could view the city **gallows**. Today, the stream no longer flows, and Las Ramblas is a broad, tree-lined street. Vendors line the street, selling books, flowers, newspapers, and even pet birds from their stalls.

Boats used for fishing and sightseeing are docked at one of Valencia's ports.

Valencia on the coast

Valencia is another bustling port city that is more than 2,000 years old. It lies about halfway down the east coast of Spain, in one of the country's most fertile regions. Orange, lemon, and peach groves surround the city. Like many other ancient cities, Valencia was once surrounded by walls. Most of these walls were torn down in the late 1800s so the city had room to grow, but two gates still stand. Cannonball holes from ancient battles mark one gate.

Seville of the south

Seville is in southwestern Spain, in Andalusia. Moors lived in Seville, Spain's fourth-largest city, for hundreds of years. Their architectural influence can still be seen today. In the old part of Seville, horseshoe-shaped archways rise above narrow, shaded streets, and the balconies of white houses overlook courtyards with lush gardens and fountains.

From anywhere in Seville, a large tower called La Giralda can be seen. La Giralda stands 300 feet (92 meters) tall, with a weathervane on its tip. It is part of a large **cathedral** called Plaza Virgen de los Reyes, which was built where a mosque, or Muslim house of worship, once stood. **Minarets** that were part of the mosque are now part of the cathedral. Some people believe that the explorer Christopher Columbus is buried in Seville's cathedral.

*The Plaza de España, in Seville, is a huge circular **plaza** that was built in 1929 for the Fair of the Americas. Along part of the **plaza** are tiled pictures that show each of Spain's provinces.*

The Puente Romana, a bridge built on ancient Roman foundations, crosses the Guadalquivir River into Córdoba.

Córdoba

Córdoba lies northeast of Seville, along the Guadalquivir River. In this small city, people can cross a Roman bridge, stand in the Great Mosque built by the Moors, and walk under a decorative arch built for King Philip II. Romans founded Córdoba in 169 B.C., but it was the Moors who declared it the capital of Spain in 756 A.D. It became a city of learning and development, boasting over 1,000 mosques and the first streetlights in all of Europe. Córdoba is now an industrial city where modern shops and cafés appear alongside older homes.

Málaga

Málaga was founded in the 1100s by people from the eastern Mediterranean, called Phoenicians, but it became prosperous when the Moors ruled Spain. Situated in the far south, near Gibraltar, it was the most important port of the region, and a strong military base. The ruins of a Moorish fortress called Alcazaba stand high on the hill overlooking the city. Some towers and walls still surround the fortress, which is now home to an **archaeology** museum. Nearby, a half-ruined **amphitheater** is evidence of the time when the Romans ruled the land. Today, Málaga serves as the main gateway to the Costa del Sol, with the principal airport for the region, and it remains an important commercial port. The main industries in this city of half-a-million people are sugar, wine, and cotton textiles.

The walls surrounding the Alcazaba can be seen from Málaga. The main parts of the Alcazaba were built by the Moors during the 700s.

From land and sea

Despite its ruggedness, over 60 percent of the land in Spain is used for farming. Wheat and barley, as well as a wide variety of fruit and vegetables, begin growing in Spain's warm climate weeks before crops begin growing in other European countries. Spain **exports** produce such as olives, oranges, peaches, tomatoes, bananas, cherries, and strawberries to these countries.

Grapes to eat and drink

Spain has over 1.5 million acres (600,000 hectares) of vineyards. People eat grapes fresh off the vine, dry them to make raisins and currants, and use them to make wine. Spain is the third-largest producer of wine after France and Italy. Spain produces a remarkable variety of wines because of the range of climates and landscapes in the country. The same kind of grapes grown in two different areas create very different tasting wines.

Two women pick grapes at a vineyard in the Pyrenees. Vineyards in Spain grow many types of grapes, such as **tempranillo, garnacha, cariñena, palomino,** *and* **albariño.**

Rioja is a region in northern Spain that produces a famous red wine called *rioja*. This wine is stored for up to three years in special oak barrels that give it a strong flavor. Spain is also famous for its sherry, which the Moors began exporting to England over 800 years ago. Sherry is a blend of wine and another alcohol, called brandy, that is made in the region surrounding the city of Jerez, in the south of Spain. The name sherry comes from the way English-speaking people mistakenly used to pronounce the Spanish name Jerez, which is really pronounced "herreth."

Olives

Spain has one of the largest olive crops in the world. Olive trees, which can live for more than two thousand years, grow throughout the country. They even grow in areas with little water because their roots spread over large distances to absorb any trace of moisture in the ground. Spaniards grow black and green olives for eating. One of the popular little snacks, called *tapas*, eaten in Spain is olives stuffed with tuna or anchovies. Spanish olive oil is also a popular export item.

(above) When olives are ripe, pickers place a large net under a tree. They drop the olives that they pick onto the net, then gather up the net and take the olives to be made into olive oil and other products.

A merchant sells fresh oranges at an outdoor market in Barcelona. Many of the oranges sold in other parts of Europe and in North America are grown in Spain.

Oranges of all types

The Moors first planted orange trees in Spain hundreds of years ago. The Spanish word for orange is *naranja*, which comes from the Arab word *naranj*. All kinds of oranges grow in Spain: big navel oranges, sweet Valencia oranges, blood oranges with their bright red pulp, clementines, and bitter Seville oranges, which are used to make a jam-like spread called marmalade.

Dates and saffron

Dates are a sweet fruit that grow on palm trees. About 200,000 date palms grow around the town of Elche, in the southeast part of the country. Elche has the largest palm grove in all of Europe! Another very special product grown in Spain is saffron. Saffron is a rare spice with a pleasant aroma, made from the dried orange **stigmas** of the crocus flower. Saffron is expensive to buy because it has to be handpicked very carefully.

The orange stigmas (top left) from crocuses (bottom) are removed and dried to make a spice called saffron.

21

Cork from trees to bottles

Spaniards make cork from the bark of the cork oak tree. First, the outer layer of bark is stripped off the tree. Then, the inner layer of bark is removed and used to make the cork. The bark can only be removed from the tree once every ten years. Stripping the tree more often would damage it, and the tree could not provide future crops. People make many useful items from cork, such as corkboards, stoppers for wine bottles, and flooring.

Making the most of water

Since much of Spain has a dry climate, Spaniards must find clever ways of growing fruits and vegetables. The *mar de plástico*, which means "sea of plastic," lies in the semi-desert region of southern Spain. The *mar de plástico* is a large area filled with plastic greenhouses where fruit grow all year round. The plastic keeps water in the air from evaporating, or drying out.

A much older way of making sure water is not wasted is the *Tribunal de las Aguas*, or Water Jury. The Water Jury meets every Thursday at noon, in Valencia. People crowd around the eight seated judges, who wear black shirts. The judges are farmers who listen to disputes about irrigation water from the Turia River. They issue small fines to people who waste water or who take water when it is not their turn. They also force farmers who damage the channels carrying the water to repair the damage. The *Tribunal* must be working, because it has been operating for over 1,000 years!

Huge sheets of cork are loaded onto the back of a truck in Andalusia.

Cattle, pigs, and sheep

Dairy cattle feed on grasses in the north of Spain. The cows supply milk and cheese, such as the sharply flavored *Manchego*, to the entire country. Other cattle are raised for meat, and some bulls are raised for the bullfighting ring. People also raise pigs throughout Spain, especially in the south, around a town called Jabugo. Pigs are used to make pork products, including a popular *tapas* called *jamón serrano*, which is made from pigs' legs.

In central Spain, people raise a breed of sheep called Merino sheep. It is often too dry for crops to grow in this region, so people allow their sheep to feed over large areas to find whatever food they can. Merino sheep are famous all over the world because of their soft wool.

A flock of Merino sheep feeds in a field in Atienza, a village in central Spain. The wool from the sheep will be used to make clothing and blankets.

From the sea

Fishers sail the water surrounding Spain, catching anchovies, sardines, cod, mackerel, hake, and tuna, as well as mussels, lobsters, clams, octopuses, and squid. The fish caught on the coasts is sold in markets all over the country. The people of Spain eat more fish and seafood per person than the people of any other country in Europe, except for Portugal. Spain also cans and exports fish to other countries.

In the past few years, Spain's fishing industry has shrunk. Many fishing boats are small and owned by families. These boats cannot compete with the newer, larger fishing boats from other countries. The fishing industry in Spain also suffers from the same problem facing many parts of the world. Overfishing has reduced the number of fish, and fishers must travel farther and farther from the coasts to catch the amount of fish they need to make a good living.

Fishers load crates full of sardines onto a dock in Alicante, on the eastern coast of Spain.

Industry and natural resources

Spain's different regions manufacture different products. People in Granada, in the south, and Murcia, in the southeast, produce rugs and carpets. Artists in Toledo, in the central part of the country, make damascene ware by gently hammering gold, silver, and copper wire into metal items, such as knives and swords, to create delicate designs. Madrileños work in high-tech industries, such as information technology and electronics. In the north of Spain, miners remove a black mineral called coal from the earth. In the south, they mine copper, lead, and zinc. In the central part of the country, they remove mercury from the largest mercury mine in the world.

(right) Part of an ocean liner is lowered onto a ramp at a shipbuilding factory in Baza, on the southern coast of Spain.

A group of miners prepare for a busy day in the Villablino Mine, in northern Spain. They wear hard hats with lights on them so they can find their way in the dark tunnels.

Cars and ships

Some of the coal mined in Spain is used to make iron and steel. With this iron and steel, companies in Spain build machine parts, washing machines, refrigerators, and even large ships. Other companies build cars, most of which they export. In Spain, more people work in the automotive industry than in any other manufacturing industry.

Tapestry is a thick, decorative material that is made by hand-weaving wool, linen, silk, and gold threads together to create beautiful patterns and designs.

Clothing and leather

Spain's thriving textile and clothing industry revolves around the region of Catalonia. Cotton grown in other parts of the country is spun here and made into cloth. Barcelona, the center of the clothing industry, is the fashion capital of Spain. Spanish factories also produce high-quality leather items, including purses and shoes.

A worker at a leather factory in Barcelona cuts different shapes out of leather. These shapes will be sewn together to make shoes.

Brightly colored ceramics

For centuries, craftspeople in Spain have made clay dishes, tiles, vases, and other ceramics with bright colors and beautiful designs. Many of the designs are Moorish and depict colorful geometric patterns. The Moors created these designs because Islam, their religion, does not allow craftspeople to represent humans in their artwork. Large ceramics factories exist near the big cities of Valencia and Seville, but many little towns make their own pottery in distinctive styles.

Many tourists

Every year, more than 50 million people from around the world come to Spain for their holidays. Tourists hike through the foothills, ski the slopes, lie on the sandy beaches, and visit some of Spain's 1,400 palaces and castles. The government has even converted some of these palaces into special hotels called *paradores*. Favorite tourist areas are the Mediterranean coast, the Balearic Islands, and the Canary Islands, as well as the larger cities. The tourist industry in Spain employs two million people. Their jobs include growing food, manufacturing souvenirs, building hotels, and working in restaurants, hotels, and tourist attractions.

(left) To make ceramic dishes, tiles, and vases, artists paint and glaze clay and then fire, or bake, it at very high temperatures.

(below) Crowds of tourists cross the Puente Romana bridge on their way to the Great Mosque in Córdoba.

26

Falling water at the dam in Alcántara is used to create electricity.

Creating energy

Some of the energy used to power Spain's factories comes from hydroelectricity, or rapidly flowing water. Spain has a large generating station on the Tagus River, at Alcántara, in the west. Other generating stations sit in the Pyrenees, producing power from rivers flowing quickly down the mountains.

Since many of its rivers do not flow quickly enough or have much water during the summer, Spain must convert other natural resources into energy. For instance, coal is burned to produce energy that runs many of Spain's generating stations. Spanish nuclear power plants create energy by splitting or combining tiny particles called atoms. A solar power plant, which generates energy from the sun, runs near Almería, on the southern coast. Windmills, which generate energy from the wind, stand on the central plains, in the region of Castilla-La Mancha. A famous Spanish story describes Don Quixote, Man of La Mancha, fighting windmills in this region because he believed that they were giants.

A damaged environment

Many European industries dump chemicals and garbage into the Mediterranean Sea or into rivers that flow into the sea. Since the Mediterranean is calm and has few tides, chemical wastes are not diluted, or spread out. As a result, the sea is becoming polluted, and many animals and plants that live there are dying. Some parts of the Spanish coast are even closed to people because of the pollution. Recently, the government introduced environmental laws to control the problem. Various environmental groups are also working to save the dying **coral reefs** in the Mediterranean Sea.

Tourism causes another kind of damage to Spain's environment. Many wild animals have lost their **habitat** because hotels, restaurants, and other tourist sites have been built where the animals once lived. New developments have also replaced historic buildings in important old cities, such as Seville and Toledo, as well as in many fishing villages, changing them forever.

Getting around

A truck drives carefully through a narrow street in Toledo, in central Spain.

Spain's many mountains, as well as its large size, make transportation routes difficult to build and repair. The Romans were the first people to construct good roads in Spain. Many of the routes Spaniards travel on today follow the path of these original Roman roads, which crumbled and decayed long ago.

Driving

Many people drive in Spain's countryside, although some still use mules to transport crops from the fields to the market. Some farmers on the Canary Islands even use camels!

In big cities, such as Madrid, Barcelona, and Valencia, most people own cars. Traffic clogs the newer streets in downtown areas, so the government has built buses and underground subway systems, called *metros*, to help with the problem. In the old quarter of many cities, the streets are too narrow to fit many vehicles. Several cities no longer allow cars on these narrow streets, just pedestrians and cyclists.

Cars and taxis crowd the Passeig de Gràcia, a street in Barcelona.

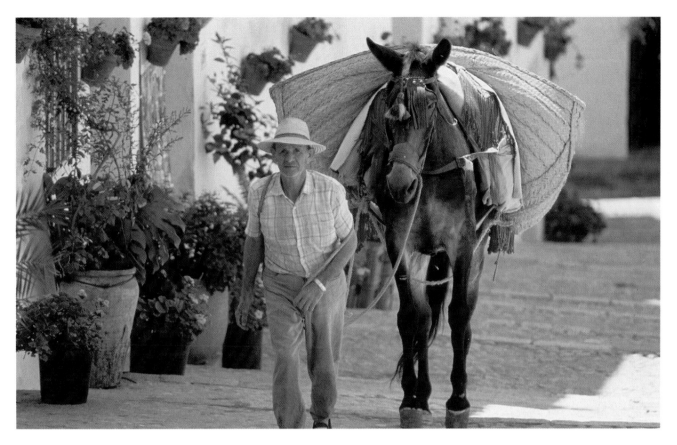

A donkey with two wicker baskets on its back carries goods to a market in Málaga.

Rugged railroads

To help people travel across the broad country, the Spanish National Railway built a very efficient railroad system. Spanish railroads have wider tracks than railroads in the rest of Europe. The wide tracks make it harder for trains to tip over on rugged, mountainous land. In the past, Spanish trains were not able to travel into France, where the tracks were narrower. Instead, passengers had to change trains at the border. Today, new Spanish trains can adjust the space between their wheels to fit on the narrower tracks.

By air and water

Airplanes owned by Spain's major airline, Iberia, fly to destinations within the country and to countries around the world. Most major Spanish cities have an airport. Traveling more slowly, ferries carrying tourists sail between the islands, as well as from Spain to the Spanish towns of Ceuta and Melilla in Morocco.

In the past, people in Spain found it easier to travel along river routes than to cross the high and rugged mountains. As a result, all beaches, rivers, and riverbeds in the country were declared public property. Today, Spaniards with rivers running through their property must still allow traffic on the river, such as people in fishing boats, onto their land. They must also allow hikers walking along the river and people herding cattle to pass through.

Two high-speed AVE trains wait for passengers to board at the Atocha Station in Madrid. "Ave" is Spanish for "bird."

Plants and animals

A variety of wild animals and plants are native to Spain. Snakes, lizards, and insects scuttle and fly through the semi-desert region in the south. Scorpions live along the eastern coast. Hedgehogs, rabbits, and hares are common in forests in the north. Spectacular butterflies, such as the oversized, two-tailed pasha, flutter through the country, and many rare birds fly through the skies.

Rich in birds

Over 400 species of birds can be spotted in Spain, especially in the south. Many are birds of prey, which hunt small mammals. The black vulture, one of Europe's largest birds of prey, and the eagle owl, the largest owl in Europe, are both native to Spain. The main reason why Spain has so many birds is its position between Europe and Africa. It is a resting place for millions of birds on their annual migration.

The century plant, which has hard spiky leaves, grows quickly. Then, when it is about ten years old, it develops a single tall flower and dies.

The golden eagle, which can be found in several parts of Spain, gets its name from the gold feathers on its head and neck. Its enormous wingspan measures 8 feet (2.4 meters) across.

Another reason for Spain's many birds is the variety of habitats in the country. Some of the most important habitats are the wetlands around rivers. More than 300,000 birds winter in the wetlands of the Coto Doñana, a **nature reserve** in southwestern Spain. Among these are about fifteen pairs of the rare Spanish imperial eagle. Up to 40,000 flamingos can sometimes be found farther inland, at the Fuente de Piedra wetlands.

Beating the heat

In areas with little rain, such as the Meseta and the mountains of southern Spain, small hardy bushes and grasses grow. Plants living here have developed ways of storing precious water. Some have thick, waxy leaves that take longer than flat leaves to dry out. Others store moisture underground in bulbs or fat roots. The umbrella pine, with its twisted and gnarled trunk, pushes its roots deep into the sand to reach the water it needs. This tree can sometimes become almost totally buried in the sand.

The Iberian lynx hunts for food at night. Its diet consists mainly of rodents and rabbits.

Plants on the Canary Islands

The Canary Islands have many small, sandy plateaus because of their volcanic origin. Two unique plants bloom in these dry areas. The dragon tree has fat branches with dense, spiky leaves all pointing up, like a giant brush. It can live for hundreds of years. The six-foot (two-meter) tall viper's bugloss plant looks like a tall, spiky cone. Its pointed leaves have a reddish tinge.

Two Iberian wolves play together at the Coto Doñana Nature Reserve.

The Coto Doñana

Hunting and habitat loss threaten many of Spain's larger wild animals. Wolves are among the most endangered animals in Spain, and fewer than 100 brown bears now live in the country. The Mediterranean monk seal, the green sea turtle, and the Hierro giant lizard are all threatened. In January 2000, the Pyrenean ibex, a kind of wild goat that lived in the upper slopes of the Pyrenees, was declared extinct, or no longer in existence.

Spain has created several nature reserves and national parks where animals, birds, and plants can live safely. The most famous of these is the Coto Doñana. Marshes, sandy dunes, low trees, and pine forests on this nature reserve provide comfortable homes to many animals. One resident here is the Iberian lynx. This rare spotted cat has fringes on its chin that look like a beard. Each lynx needs its own territory, which is why disappearing habitat has endangered the animal.

Glossary

amphitheater An oval or round theater with levels of seats rising from a stage where contests and public performances are held

archaeology The study of buildings and artifacts from the past

autonomy The right of a group of people to govern itself

capital A city where the government of a state or country is located

cathedral A large church

coral reef A ridge of coral

custom Something that a group of people has done for so long that it becomes an important part of their way of life

descendant A person who can trace his or her family roots to a certain family or group

export To sell goods to another country

fertile Able to produce abundant crops or vegetation

flamenco A rhythmic style of music and dance

gallows A wooden structure used to hang and execute criminals

Gulf Stream A warm ocean current that flows through the Atlantic Ocean

habitat An area or environment in which plants or animals are normally found

historian A person who studies history

humid Moist or damp

irrigation The process of supplying water to land

limestone A rock used for building

minaret A tall, slender tower from which a person calls Muslim people to prayer

Muslim A person who believes in Islam, a religion based on the teachings of God, whom Muslims call *Allah*, and his prophet Muhammad

nature reserve A park where wildlife is protected from hunters and is observed by scientists and tourists

outcrop A piece of rock that sticks out of the ground

peninsula An area of land that is surrounded by water on three sides

plateau An area of flat land that is higher than the surrounding land

port A place where ships load and unload cargo

promenade A public area where people stroll

shale A type of rock that forms over many years, when clay, mud, or sand is put under great pressure

sovereignty The supreme power or authority of one country over an area of land in another country

stigma The part of a plant where pollen is deposited

Stone Age The earliest known period of any human culture, characterized by the use of tools and weapons made of stone

territory An area of land or water within a country ruled by an outside country

Index